CW01307301

How to Overcome the Fear of Driving (Amaxophobia) Strategies and Useful Tips

OLTRE I PROPRI LIMITI

Table of Contents

INTRODUCTION
PHOBIAS: A SIMPLE BUT IMPORTANT DISCUSSION
AMAXOPHOBIA
MY EXPERIENCE

HOW TO OVERCOME THE FEAR OF DRIVING: TIPS AND STRATEGIES. WHAT TO DO
CONCLUSIONS
CONTACTS

INTRODUCTION

Dear reader,

I have decided to write this book to share my experience regarding the issue of amaxophobia (literally "fear of driving") and the numerous subjective and social consequences that arise from it, so that anyone going through the same identical difficulty can find support, inspiration, comfort, or simply a comparison regarding their situation, allowing them to draw a guideline to follow in resolving the issue, or at least making it more acceptable or manageable.

It's a way of saying that you are not alone in this problem and that what you are experiencing right now, I have also experienced before you and, like us, hundreds of thousands of people around the world over the years.

Over time, I have realized, through direct experience with statements, comparisons, and interviews, that many of us live with this discomfort, which is far more common than one might think or what people show, due to customs or social conventions that limit the exposure of what is not considered "normal" by society, but is indeed normal, considering that everyone, sooner or later, at least once in their "driving careers," has faced unpleasant situations they would have gladly avoided, as they generate anxious states perceived as such and with varying degrees of tolerance.

But what leads one person, compared to another, to develop such debilitating anxiety that it traps them in a state of perpetual anguish?

Starting from this question, and seeking a satisfactory answer, I embarked on the writing of this text because I believe that finding the focus behind this question could be an excellent starting point to delve deeply into the problem, highlighting what nourishes and feeds it, even if of course there cannot be a one-size-fits-all opinion since each of us is an individual in themselves, with their own peculiarities, ideas, beliefs, stories, anxieties, and fears. Moreover, every life path is different, just as the various experiences that have conditioned and shaped it over time are different, even if they have led to the same (or very similar) consequences.

Thus, the most logical discussion inevitably shifts to this other track, that is, starting from these consequences to find a general thread in which various cases can fit, to expose the main motivations that may underlie them, so that we can face and resolve them once and for all, whether the fear is a source or an effect of something more rooted in us.

Having a discussion on this topic was the reason that drove me, back in 2017, to open a YouTube channel so that I could freely talk about the problem I was experiencing, which at the time seemed almost insurmountable to me.
I needed guidance and, at the same time, wanted to understand how many people were living in my condition, to feel less alone, what strategies to implement, and what path to follow to cope with

and best overcome this fear.

To my surprise, I quickly realized that we were indeed many experiencing this discomfort, many more than I would have ever imagined, regardless of age, gender, or social background.

There was the newly licensed girl terrified of traffic, the family man who hadn't driven in years, the woman who had gotten her license two decades earlier but had never gotten behind the wheel for fear of hitting pedestrians, and even the boy who was driven everywhere by his mother whenever a car was needed.

From this, the idea emerged to leave my Telegram

contact and personal email so that anyone who wanted to reach out to me regarding amaxophobia could do so. This remains true to this day.

Over the years, many hundreds of people have reached out to me for advice or simply to discuss this discomfort.

Now I have decided to close the loop by writing this book, providing a useful resource with all the most important knowledge needed to tackle phobia in general and how to overcome this particular fear.

Through my experience, I hope that what is

written here can provide the necessary motivation, as well as open the eyes to aspects that perhaps consciously or unconsciously those who suffer from such discomfort may not be able to confront or understand correctly, because "clouded" by a problem they don't know how to manage or simply because they do not have the necessary tools to do so.

The goal is precisely to provide these tools in the clearest and simplest way possible, to be accessible to everyone.

This is why I will not dwell on overly technical discussions or unnecessary verbosity, but rather aim to be as clear and concise as possible, explaining all the mechanisms that come into play when living in such a situation, what to do to prevent it from becoming too burdensome over time, and how to take action to eradicate it at its roots once and for all from one's cognitive and behavioral processes, as well as explaining which attitudes, conversely, should not be taken to avoid strengthening it.

PHOBIAS: A SIMPLE BUT IMPORTANT DISCUSSION

In psychology, the term "phobia" refers to an irrational fear that is so intense regarding certain situations, objects, places, activities, people, or animals that it severely hinders the life of the individual suffering from it, as they are unable to confront it in a proper manner. More specifically, it is a type of anxiety disorder that causes anxiety to manifest in extreme and exaggerated ways, leading the phobic individual to experience a series of physical and psychological symptoms that traumatize them to such an extent that they avoid the specific situation.

Avoidance is one of the mechanisms our mind, and consequently our body, employs when it feels threatened by an external event deemed dangerous. This defense mechanism, essentially a behavioral strategy, leads the person exhibiting it to refuse to confront situations, subjects, animals, or objects that induce distress. It is precisely the withdrawal from exposure to the triggering event that characterizes adaptive behavior, which is appropriate when the danger is real. However, it becomes a defense mechanism to protect oneself from a mental state considered intolerable, and therefore to be avoided, when the perception of danger is disproportionate to the event itself.

A person who experiences extreme fear thus creates a comfort zone around them where they feel safe, at least mentally achieving this illusion, believing they can limit any potential negative effects on their personal sphere should they occur in reality. This behavior can stem from both external factors and internal factors such as thoughts or moods.

In fact, emotions are the core of this dysfunctional attitude because it is a specific (or rather, an attempted) way to better control them and not be overwhelmed by them. This illustrates how avoidance is a defensive mechanism typical of anxiety disorders, as it involves avoiding contact with the triggering event.

The more anxious someone is, the more they flee from confronting a particular situation, convincing themselves that it is justified to do so, as it reaffirms their belief that they can do nothing but distance themselves from that thing or activity that generates anxiety. This creates a vicious cycle that is difficult to escape, especially when it becomes entrenched in the behavioral spectrum, particularly if the person begins to adapt to that avoidant situation.

In other words, it becomes a strategy implemented whenever there is a feeling of danger, with the specific goal of controlling the emotions experienced, leading to an acceptance of that condition and a refusal to face it. Thus, it becomes entrenched over time, making it increasingly difficult to root it out from one's mind, particularly when there is no known alternative or when the option of confronting it is not regarded as feasible or advantageous. The trigger of all this is the anxiety resulting from an external event perceived as dangerous.

Anxiety (from the ancient Greek "angere," meaning to tighten) is an emotional state that characterizes all humans and animals in their personal or social behaviors. Essentially, there are two types of anxiety: normal, which carries a positive value, and pathological, which is limiting for the life of those who suffer from it. Normal anxiety is that state of mind which warns us of danger, preserving our lives, allowing humanity to safeguard itself and survive throughout history, facilitating the evolution of our species. It is a part of our lives and activates in situations where being alert is appropriate. Thus, it has a positive value for personal or collective protection when viewed from a functional perspective.

Pathological anxiety, on the other hand, is the type that limits the individual's adaptability because it forces them to live in a constant state of discomfort and anguish, particularly the feeling of imminent danger, that is, a catastrophic event that is believed to likely occur shortly. It is clear how such a state of mind is detrimental to those who endure it and how it can condition life itself, especially when that life is lived primarily in terms of an emotional aspect that tends to restrict it.

There are two main ways that each human or animal reacts when feeling threatened, represented by the "fight or flight" mechanism. When we perceive a danger, our instinct tells us to confront the situation in two ways; either by fighting back, thus facing what we believe is about to attack us, or, conversely, by fleeing from it.

In this mode of acting, we express primitive behavior. Indeed, when we are compelled to activate this mechanism (unconsciously, unwillingly), we are not much different from animals; just as a bear cornered by a poacher chooses to retreat or confront them with a counter-attack, risking everything, we act similarly. However, the difference is that the situations we consider dangerous and potentially life-threatening are often nothing more than products of our imagination, mere mental projections.

This illustrates the dichotomy between the past and the present, highlighted by the role anxiety played in our evolution when we had to flee from ferocious animals to preserve our safety and that of our loved ones, enabling progress as a species over time. In contrast, today that same anxiety remains in our mental processes, primal yet resurfacing due to the stressors it perceives, even though it no longer holds the same significance as it once did, given the changed environmental and social context in which we live.

Those same instincts, which once represented fleeing from a predator to save one's life, now translate into stress signals from the outside, such as crossing the street without being hit by a car, or avoiding burning the chicken we put in the oven.

In the former case, anxiety played a fundamental and decisive role in survival, essential to the development of human life, while in the latter case, when it becomes pathological, it has a regressive effect on the individual who comprises the collective.

Having clarified this point, it can be easily inferred that anxiety, by its very essence, originates from this mechanism that activates all physiological responses arising from neurovegetative processes, necessary to initiate the action of either fighting or fleeing.

The signals that reach us from the brain include:

Increased heart rate;

Heightened breathing rhythm;

Trembling and sweating;

Tightness in the stomach and nausea;

Muscle tension;

Pupil dilation;

Dry mouth;

Dizziness;

Sense of oppression in the chest;

Feelings of fainting or imminent death.

When we find ourselves in a stressful situation, in fact, our cerebral cortex sends a message to the sympathetic nervous system to prepare the body for immediate behavior that will need to be enacted shortly. After a quick assessment of the risks and benefits associated with a specific action, or if no other solution is found, we will act according to the two paths described earlier.

The state of alarm that results is what leads to phobia because if this state diminishes over time, simple anxiety remains as such, causing no

significant problems except temporary ones.
However, if it becomes chronic, it will turn into stress, a perpetual state of discomfort that can trigger excessive responses when there is an overload of emotional, cognitive, or social tasks that are difficult for the human mind to manage.

In this case, the so-called Gaussian curve comes into play, a mathematical concept that can be well related to the real world, especially to our psychological side. There is, in fact, an acceptable baseline level of stress. When we are within the limits of this line, our emotional state tolerates that level of tension well, even though it may reach higher points following the curve's trajectory. Nothing remarkable, as when it reaches those peaks, we experience anxiety more intensely, but temporarily. The concept that characterizes the parabola is precisely that of temporariness because, being an ascending/descending curve, once it reaches a limit, at its peak, it will inevitably begin to descend, following its physiological development characterized by a wave-like pattern, which is not constant over time but always derived from an emotional state perceived as calm or, on the contrary, alarming.

Upon reaching the peak, the crisis point, it will again start to fluctuate downwards, towards recovery. If there are further external stressors, it will rise again; otherwise, it will fall to tolerable levels, and so forth until the mind and body adapt to the response they need to give. However, this adaptation is not always optimal.

In many cases, it gives rise to an immense feeling of discomfort, perceived as such, that never seems to end, as that peak is represented by panic. One experiences a state where anxiety transforms into panic, which our nervous system poorly tolerates: sensations of fainting, losing control, going insane, a lack of air, a desire to flee far from that situation of imminent death/catastrophe.

Anyone who has experienced a panic attack at least once in their life knows well how it manifests and how difficult it is to manage in practice. The issue, as previously stated, is not so much the panic attack itself because, as we have seen, it has a beginning and an end (usually a time period ranging from 5 to at most 10 minutes), but it's when this state of discomfort becomes chronic that the real problem arises. In fact, if one lives in an emotional state consistently at the peak of the famous Gaussian curve, one will eventually expand that state of anxiety. Thus, it will just take a minimal event (action, situation, or thought) that exacerbates the already precarious situation, that anxious starting point (which has now become the zero point) already constantly high, leading to crossing that limit no longer tolerable and touching panic, i.e., the extreme manifestation of fear.

During a panic attack, physical symptoms intensify and are perceived as tragic, creating a vicious circle that merely self-feeds and, to some extent, legitimizes itself. Therefore, thoughts arise that constantly repeat in the mind of the sufferer such as "I will die," "I will lose control," "I will faint," and so on. Panic, then, is the extreme manifestation of anxiety, that is, normal bodily reactions due to the latter, but perceived as deadly and irreparable. If panic is the exacerbation of anxiety, phobia is nothing more than the intensification of fear that derives from the first two.

An incorrect assessment of the event, in relation to an invisible but imminent danger that is perceived, leads the individual suffering from it to feel nonexistent threats, triggering the fight-or-flight response even when it is completely unnecessary because it is unreal. This process can be described as "anticipatory anxiety," that is, the feeling of anguish and fear that arises at the mere thought of having to face a perceived dangerous or distressing situation in the future.

It therefore stems from a prediction, an idea, a fantasy based on personal thoughts that project the subject into the future, in that specific situation, but creating in their mind all the worst possible and imaginable scenarios, which in turn only serve to feed the same initial anxious state. In this way, the person will begin to avoid all places, people, or situations that lead to that discomfort because it is conceived as impossible to endure and live through, in short, intolerable.

This passive-regressive attitude inevitably limits the life of the sufferer because the individual will always live in a state of alertness, with the idea and conviction that something unpleasant will surely happen in that forthcoming projection which they will not be able to face adequately.

It begins with an "if" that will concatenate with others: "if I do this thing and then this other thing happens," or "if I go to that place and that situation arises, I won't know how to act," etc. The symptoms are similar to those of generalized anxiety in the immediate situation, such as tachycardia, nausea, the sensation of fainting, etc., while cognitive symptoms may even become more pronounced, such as mental confusion, rumination of thought, irritability, loss of hope, or sleep disturbances caused by constant, decidedly obsessive negative thoughts.

This type of anxiety is linked to specific states that a person no longer wants to experience, such as panic attacks. If a panic attack occurs in a specific place or moment, it is very likely that the individual who experienced it will create an association between that place or event and the sensation they had to endure in that particular circumstance, attempting to avoid it as much as possible. Sometimes, it may stem from negative cognitions—thoughts or a distorted idea we have of ourselves that we convince ourselves is real, even if it is far from the actual truth.

An example is feeling inadequate in facing a situation and believing that, if it were to actually arise, we would not be able to handle it well. Other cases of anticipatory anxiety can pertain to social phobia, i.e., the fear of being in social contexts and having to act, such as speaking in public, finding it difficult even at the mere thought of having to do it; hypochondria, i.e., the fear of having illnesses or falling ill in some way, perceiving normal bodily reactions as imminent signs of potentially deadly situations; or even post-traumatic stress, which is related to an experienced trauma that one believes may reoccur in the future.

Therefore, anticipatory anxiety is nothing more than an anxious state in which our mind creates a whole series of catastrophic projections, most often without concrete or real foundations, but which only serve to fuel themselves, consequently leading to the fear and evasion that results from it.

This is the common denominator of all the phobias that exist in the world, which are definitely numerous, indicating that human beings predominantly tend to live in projections, in an effort to control in their mind potential deadly external situations so as to put into action, in advance (anticipating the effects), survival strategies. In other words, it's a way of acting to preserve one's own life that has always worked in the past.

The survival instinct, therefore, is the core, and the

fear of falling ill or dying is the direct consequence.

Despite the countless phobias that exist in the world, it's worth mentioning a few to understand how widespread and still little known they are. Among many, we find:

Ablutophobia: fear of washing or bathing.

Acarophobia: fear of itching.

Acataphobia: fear of dirt.

Acerophobia: fear of sourness.

Acluophobia: fear of darkness.

Acrophobia: fear of heights.

Acousticophobia: fear of sounds.

Aeroacrophobia: fear of high places.

Aerophobia: fear of air.

Aeronausiphobia: fear of vomiting due to air travel.

Afefobia: fear of contact, of being touched.

Agiophobia: fear of saints, sacred things.

Aglophobia: fear of pain.

Agoraphobia: fear of open spaces.

Agrafobia: fear of sexual abuse.

Agrizoophobia: fear of wild animals.

Agyrophobia: fear of streets or crossing streets.

Aichmophobia: fear of sharp objects.

Ailurophobia: fear of cats.

Albuminurophobia: fear of kidney disease.

Alectorophobia: fear of chickens.

Algophobia: fear of suffering.

Alliumphobia: fear of garlic.

Allodoxaphobia: fear of opinions different from one's own.

Amathophobia: fear of making mistakes.

Amatophobia: fear of dust.

Amaxophobia: fear of driving a car.

Ambulophobia: fear of walking.

Amnesiphobia: fear of suffering from amnesia.

Amychophobia: fear of scratches.

Anablephobia: fear of looking up.

Anchilophobia: fear of the immobility of a joint.

Androphobia: fear of men.

Anemophobia: fear of wind.

Anginophobia: fear of choking.

Anglophobia: fear of England and English people.

Angrophobia: fear of being hungry.

Antlofobia: fear of floods.

Anthophobia: fear of flowers.

Anthropophobia: fear of people and social contacts.

Anuptaphobia: fear of remaining unmarried.

Apeirophobia: fear of infinity.

Apiphobia: fear of bees.

Apotemnophobia: fear of amputees.

Arachibutyrophobia: fear of peanut butter sticking to the roof of the mouth.

Arachnophobia: fear of spiders.

Arithmeticophobia: fear of numbers.

Asymmetriphobia: fear of asymmetrical things.

Astenophobia: fear of fainting or feeling weak.

Astraphobia: fear of thunder and lightning.

Ataxophobia: fear of ataxia.

Athazagoraphobia: fear of being forgotten or ignored, or of forgetting.

Atephobia: fear of ruins.

Atelophobia: fear of imperfection.

Atomosophobia: fear of atomic explosions.

Atychiphobia: fear of failure.

Aulophobia: fear of flutes.

Aurophobia: fear of gold.

Auroraphobia: fear of dawn.

Autofobia: fear of being alone or of oneself.

Autodysmorphophobia: fear of being ugly.

Automatonophobia: fear of anything that represents a human being.

Automysophobia: fear of being dirty.

Aviophobia: fear of flying.

Bacillophobia: fear of microbes.

Bacteriophobia: fear of bacteria.

Ballistophobia: fear of bullets.

Barophobia: fear of gravity.

Basophobia: fear of falling.

Batophobia: fear of depth and heights.

Batonophobia: fear of plants.

Batrachophobia: fear of frogs and amphibians.

Bibliophobia: fear of books.

Biophobia: fear of living with humans or animals.

Blennophobia: fear of slimy things.

Bogeymanphobia: fear of goblins.

Bolshevikophobia: fear of Bolsheviks.

Bribolophobia: fear of bribes.

Bromidrophobia: fear of body odors.

Brontophobia: fear of thunder.

Bufonophobia: fear of toads.

Cacophobia: fear of ugliness.

Cainophobia: fear of new things or ideas.

Calligynephobia: fear of beautiful women.

Cancerophobia: fear of getting cancer.

Cardiophobia: fear of heart diseases.

Carnophobia: fear of meat.

Catagelophobia: fear of being ridiculed and laughed at.

Catapedaphobia: fear of jumping.

Catisophobia: fear of sitting down.

Chaetophobia: fear of hair.

Cheimophobia: fear of cold.

Chemophobia: fear of chemicals.

Cherophobia: fear of happiness.

Chinophobia: fear of snow.

Chiraptophobia: fear of being touched.

Chorophobia: fear of dancing.

Chrometophobia: fear of money.

Cibophobia: fear of food.

Cyclophobia: fear of bicycles.

Cinematophobia: fear of movement.

Cynophobia: fear of dogs.

Claustrophobia: fear of closed spaces.

Cleisiophobia: fear of being locked up.

Cleptophobia: fear of stealing.

Climacophobia: fear of stairs.

Clinophobia: fear of going to bed.

Cnidophobia: fear of jellyfish.

Coimetrophobia: fear of cemeteries.

Coitophobia: fear of sexual intercourse.

Colerophobia: fear of anger.

Cometophobia: fear of comets.

Coprostasophobia: fear of constipation.

Coprophobia: fear of feces.

Coulrophobia: fear of clowns.

Counterphobia: the pleasure of a phobic person in seeking frightening situations.

Cremnophobia: fear of cliffs.

Cryophobia: fear of cold.

Cristallophobia: fear of glass.

Chromatophobia: fear of colors.

Chronophobia: fear of time.

Chronometrophobia: fear of clocks.

Cyberphobia: fear of computers.

Cymophobia: fear of waves or swaying movements.

Cypriphobia: fear of prostitutes or sexually transmitted diseases.

Daemonophobia: fear of demons.

Decidophobia: fear of making decisions.

Defecaloesophobia: fear of painful bowel movements.

Deipnophobia: fear of dining or conversing at dinner.

Dementophobia: fear of insanity.

Demophobia: fear of crowds.

Dendrophobia: fear of trees.

Dentophobia: fear of dentists.

Dermatophobia: fear of skin lesions or diseases.

Dextrophobia: fear of objects to the right of the

body.

Diabetophobia: fear of diabetes.

Didascaleinophobia: fear of going to school.

Dichephobia: fear of justice.

Dinophobia: fear of dizziness.

Diplofobia: fear of seeing double.

Dipsofobia: fear of drinking.

Disablophobia: fear of undressing in front of someone.

Dysmorphophobia or Quasimodophobia: fear of being or appearing deformed.

Domatophobia: fear of houses, of being inside a house or in the vicinity of a house.

Doraphobia: fear of fur.

Dromophobia: fear of means of transportation.

Dystychophobia: fear of accidents.

Ecclesiophobia: fear of churches.

Ecophobia: fear of being home alone.

Hedonophobia: fear of experiencing physical pleasure.

Eisoptrophobia: fear of mirrors.

Electrophobia: fear of electricity.

Eleutherophobia: fear of freedom.

Heliofobia: fear of the sun.

Emetophobia: fear of vomiting.

Hemophobia: fear of blood.

Elmintophobia: fear of worms.

Enetophobia: fear of pins.

Enissophobia: fear of having committed an unforgivable sin.

Enophobia: fear of wine.

Enochlophobia: fear of crowds.

Entomophobia: fear of insects.

Eosophobia: fear of dawn.

Epistaxisophobia: fear of nosebleeds.

Epistemophobia: fear of knowledge.

Equinophobia: fear of horses.

Eremophobia: fear of being oneself or of loneliness.

Erythrophobia: fear of the color red.

Ergasiophobia: fear of work.

Erotophobia: fear of sexual love.

Herpetophobia: fear of reptiles or creeping animals.

Heterophobia: fear of the opposite sex.

Euphorophobia: fear of hearing good news.

Eurotophobia: fear of female genitalia.

Phagophobia: fear of eating.

Phalacrophobia: fear of baldness.

Phallophobia: fear of the penis.

Pharmacophobia: fear of medications.

Philophobia: fear of falling in love.

Phobophobia: fear of fear.

Phonophobia: fear of sounds.

Photophobia: fear of light.

Francophobia: fear or hostility towards France or

the French.

Gamophobia: fear of marriage or of getting married.

Gephyrophobia: fear of bridges.

Genufobia: fear of knees.

Gerontophobia: fear of aging.

Gymnophobia: fear of nudity.

Gynophobia: fear of women.

Glossophobia: fear of speaking (in public).

Gonophobia: fear of corners of buildings.

Graphophobia: fear of writing.

Iatrophobia: fear of doctors.

Hydrophobia: fear of water.

Hydrophobophobia: fear of rabies.

Hygrophobia: fear of humidity.

Hypnophobia: fear of sleeping.

Ichthyophobia: fear of fish.

Keraunophobia: fear of thunder.

Lalophobia: fear of speaking.

Lepidophobia: fear of leprosy.

Leukophobia: fear of the color white.

Lilapsophobia: fear of storms.

Limnophobia: fear of lakes.

Lisophobia: fear of leaving things unresolved.

Logophobia: fear of words.

Maniafobia: fear of mental illness.

Mastigophobia: fear of being punished.

Megalophobia: fear of large things.

Melanophobia: fear of the color black.

Melophobia: fear of music.

Meningitophobia: fear of diseases related to the brain.

Menophobia: fear of menstruation.

Metallophobia: fear of metals.

Mycophobia: fear of mushrooms.

Microphobia: fear of small things.

Myrmecophobia: fear of ants.

Misophobia: fear of contamination from contact with foreign bodies.

Mnemophobia: fear of memories.

Monophobia: fear of solitude.

Monopathophobia: fear of becoming ill related to

a specific, determined disease.

Mottephobia: fear of moths.

Musophobia: fear of mice.

Necrophobia: fear of death.

Nephophobia: fear of clouds.

Neophobia: fear of novelties.

Nyctophobia: fear of the dark.

Nosocomephobia: fear of hospitals.

Nosophobia: fear of becoming ill.

Obesophobia: fear of gaining weight.

Obophobia: fear of homeless people.

Ophidiophobia: fear of snakes.

Ombrophobia: fear of rain.

Ommetaphobia: fear of eyes.

Homophobia: fear of homosexual people.

Ornithophobia: fear of birds.

Pagophobia: fear of ice.

Panophobia: fear of everything.

Papyrophobia: fear of paper.

Parasitophobia: fear of parasites.

Parthenophobia: fear of virgins.

Pathophobia: fear of diseases.

Pediculophobia: fear of lice.

Pedophobia: fear of children.

Peniaophobia: fear of poverty.

Pyrophobia: fear of fire.

Placophobia: fear of tombs.

Plutophobia: fear of wealth.

Pluviophobia: fear of rain.

Pogonophobia: fear of beards.

Polypophobia: fear of many things (a collection of phobias).

Potamophobia: fear of rivers.

Radiophobia: fear of radiation.

Rupophobia: fear of dirt.

Sciophobia: fear of shadows.

Scoleciphobia: fear of worms.

Scopophobia: fear of being looked at.

Scopulophobia: fear of submerged rocks.

Scotomaphobia: fear of becoming blind.

Scriptohobia: fear of writing.

Selenophobia: fear of the moon.

Sesquipedalophobia: fear of long words.

Sexophobia: fear of sex.

Spheksophobia: fear of wasps.

Siderophobia: fear of stars.

Siderodromophobia: fear of moving metallic objects.

Symmetrophobia: fear of symmetrical things.

Sinophobia: fear of China, Chinese people.

Sociophobia: fear of social relationships.

Spigolophobia: fear of sharp objects.

Selachophobia: fear of sharks.

Tachophobia: fear of speed.

Tafophobia: fear of being buried alive.

Thalassophobia: fear of the sea.

Thanatophobia: obsessive fear of death.

Taurophobia: fear of bulls.

Technophobia: fear of technology.

Thermophobia: fear of heat.

Tomophobia: fear of cuts and surgical procedures.

Topophobia: fear of certain places.

Toxophobia: fear of being poisoned.

Traumatophobia: fear of injury.

Trichophobia: fear of hair.

Triskaidekaphobia: fear of the number 13.

Tropophobia: fear of moving.

Uranophobia: fear of the sky.

Urophobia: fear of urine and urinating.

Vaccinophobia: fear of vaccinations.

Venustraphobia: fear of beautiful women.

Verbophobia: fear of words.

Verminophobia: fear of germs.

Xanthophobia: fear of the color yellow.

Xenoglossophobia: fear of foreign languages.

Xenophobia: fear of foreigners.

Xerophobia: fear of drought.

Xylophobia: fear of wooden objects.

Zoophobia: fear of animals.

Even though some of these fears may seem quite bizarre or at least singular, this long list provides a clear understanding of how prevalent fear is in the human mind and how much it tends to influence our daily actions, in some cases even compromising the quality of life itself.

AMAXOPHOBIA

The term "amaxophobia," derived from the union of two ancient Greek words, namely "hám axa" meaning "cart" and "phobos" meaning "fear," indicates the fear of driving a particular means of transportation and more specifically refers to the discomfort of driving a car.

There can be various motivations behind this anxiety disorder, such as a traumatic event experienced directly or indirectly, related to road accidents or not, low self-esteem, and a limited perception of one's own ability to confront particular driving situations, such as driving on the highway, on unfamiliar roads, in traffic, or in situations that generate anxiety, like crossing bridges and tunnels. Additionally, it could stem from social phobia, particularly in the situation of being at the mercy of events and the judgment of others if one fails to adequately manage a certain circumstance, such as parking correctly or getting stuck on an incline with the engine dying while cars behind start honking.

A series of catastrophic thoughts, therefore, fuel this discomfort, causing the individual who suffers from it to feel increasingly inadequate and diminished, especially if characterized by a perfectionist spirit that shakes their self-assurances in practice.

As can be easily inferred, distorted projections are

created that increase anxiety, leading to panic and subsequent phobia, represented by the general malaise experienced in the moments before driving, during driving, or afterwards. The person who passively endures these sensations tries to escape them, as is the case with any other phobia. They do not want to find themselves in that specific situation because they perceive it as intolerable, and therefore, instead of facing it, they tend to avoid it. This same avoidance, as seen, only serves to feed the fear itself and create a vicious cycle, like a dog chasing its tail.

In this way, it becomes something extremely

debilitating because it prevents the amaxophobic individual from leading a normal life as they would like, especially if this thought becomes an obsession, forcing them to depend entirely on others (friends and family) or on public transport, thereby losing the full autonomy and freedom of their choices and actions.

The individual then feels incapable of reacting to the problem, exaggerating it, and being sucked into its vortex, which becomes an obsession, a constant thought in their mind that never leaves them, undermining their certainties and self-esteem as a human being, making them feel unworthy or unequal to others who do not face this problem. Often, they will end up comparing themselves to those who do not experience this discomfort, mortifying and belittling themselves as individuals, which fuels a strong sense of frustration regarding it. They almost regress to an infantile state.

For these reasons, they tend to feel ashamed and refrain from discussing it with others, especially friends or family, for fear of the judgment they might receive, thereby doubting their own human worth. This judgment originates from within themselves, but they project it onto others and ultimately identify with it.

In amaxophobia, as previously mentioned, a crucial role that underlies its development may be represented by an external triggering cause, among the various ones mentioned (or others depending on the experiences of the individual in question), low self-esteem, but above all by anticipatory anxiety that only reinforces those ideas that subsequently develop, starting from an external or internal input, as the case may be. The individual thus enters into a mental state of discomfort even, and especially, when the situation has not yet occurred, simply at the thought of driving, being in a car alone or with others, or under the judgment of these others who could emotionally hurt them, whether they are acquaintances or not. This results in difficulty making clear decisions, leading to mistakes that, in turn, legitimize the fear.

Amaxophobia thus triggers all the physical and psychological symptoms arising from the fight or flight mechanism. All of this occurs through a "mechanical" process that our body activates. The autonomic nervous system acts unconsciously, regulating heart rate, digestion, breathing, etc. This mechanism controls the fight or flight response through the sympathetic and parasympathetic nervous systems. It all originates from the amygdala, a gland located in the brain that perceives and creates human emotions, specifically fear, immediately detecting any potential alarm signal and generating a response that acts on the hypothalamus, which, in a chain reaction, in turn involves the pituitary gland that produces hormones preparing the body for action (either fight or flight). In a normal vital system, it provides the necessary stimuli for a physiological response to fear, while it becomes harmful in an excessively stressed system. Chronic stress, in fact, causes harm to the person both at the very moment it manifests and to the brain in the long term because, over the long term, it causes a series of dysfunctions such as memory loss, misjudgment of the contexts in which they operate or live, and deficits in self-control, etc.

When extreme, stress generates impulses that send the nervous system into overdrive, no longer able to correctly distinguish what a real danger is and what is merely the product of a personal fantasy. It confuses the very mechanism of adaptation to stress when the latter overwhelms and becomes panic.

As seen, this phobia touches on various spheres: emotional, cognitive, physiological, and behavioral, causing a psychological block from which it is difficult to detach. This is because people with amaxophobia see traffic, pedestrians, cars, or other drivers as a danger to themselves, or conversely, see themselves as a danger to others, not feeling capable of managing a potential risky situation in which they might hypothetically find themselves. Thus arise the typical thoughts derived from fears: "I won't be able to react," "I will lose control," "I will have an accident," etc.

The hyper-control stemming from personalities

unable to contemplate the unforeseen and the repetition of ritual actions to reassure themselves only serve to fuel the fear itself, leading to a resignation in facing it. Indeed, some personality traits are responsible for the vulnerability of these individuals. A rigid, perfectionistic, and controlling way of thinking, low self-esteem, and cohabitation with other phobic disorders are the most common traits. When speaking in general terms, one can begin to understand how widespread this issue is in the world. Although it is not yet very well-known as a term, it is certainly more widespread than one might think as a behavioral dysfunction.

Indeed, according to a study conducted by MAPFRE (Amaxophobia - Fear of Driving), 33% of the population suffers from this phobia. Of these, 64% are women and 36% are men. Moreover, 18% experience such paralyzing fear that it completely prevents them from getting in the car and driving.

MY EXPERIENCE

I have always been an anxious person. In fact, since I was little, one could say even in my earliest childhood, I learned to live with anxiety. I soon had to face the harsh reality of things, namely going to school—a place that felt extremely dreadful to me, or at least perceived as such. I didn't like being around other kids or adults at all. I hated being confined within four walls, in a classroom full of individuals I didn't know, feeling at the mercy of events. I didn't feel safe. I didn't even like the teachers; they were not very loving or understanding.

From all those negative feelings I experienced, I began to develop the first symptoms of what would later become a full-blown social phobia. Every morning, before going to school, I felt nauseous, often vomited, experienced various gastrointestinal problems, and constantly felt sad and uncomfortable. Especially during lunchtime, as I had always had issues eating with strangers; I felt judged and inadequate, as if everyone were staring at me, causing my stomach to clench in reaction. This feeling of inadequacy in being around others made me start to change my character compared to the child I was outside of what I saw as a kind of prison.

Another unpleasant sensation that often accompanied me, which later became crucial in my personality development, was feeling abandoned. It wasn't the first separation I experienced from my family, as my mother worked outside the home, and my father was never a present figure in my life. Thus, my sisters and I had learned from a young age to rely on ourselves. We were raised by our grandparents, and this was a tough blow to accept because I felt a greater separation from them, which made me feel like that bond was somehow breaking.

I thus lived in a state of heightened agitation stemming from anxiety. So, from a very young age, I became aware (consciously or not, given my young age) of being predisposed to suffer all the effects produced by this issue.

As mentioned, this way of being and acting was likely a reflection of a dysfunctional family situation, one that lacked care, in which I found myself living, where I had few points of reference, and those that appeared were not always positive or the best.

My parents often argued, and there was always an atmosphere of tension in the household, especially psychologically. I often feared expressing even a single idea because I already knew it would be taken as a pretext to start a war within the family. This situation lingered over time, marking me as a person. It made me very uncomfortable.

From my house, there often came screams and shouts, arguments of various natures and intensities. From those fights, I felt an infinite sadness, as well as shame, because the neighbors could only hear my relatives arguing, whether it was my mother with my father, or my grandfather with my mother, and so on.

I began, therefore, to accumulate many unpleasant feelings over time, to internalize them and carry them within me. Sometimes I felt almost as if I were the one to blame for everything.

My father, as mentioned, was completely absent from my life, so I missed a strong paternal figure who could make me feel safe and protected since my mother was always a very anxious person who transmitted a lot of her anxieties and fears to me, often stemming from the excessive love she always felt for her children, which she wanted to preserve in a glass case forever.

So, on one side, I had a person who was never there, in any occasion or circumstance, and on the other, a person who transmitted her anxiety in every way. A lovely mix for raising a child full of insecurities and fears.

The remaining parental figures were my grandparents, but they were not always positive. My grandfather, for all his goodness and affection, occasionally had fits of rage (stemming from a not always easy past), while my grandmother was an extremely loving figure but also passive. I remember constantly feeling my grandfather's judgment, rarely feeling adequate to him, not considering myself strong enough in character.

Childhood is the most critical period in the development of an individual's personality; when solid foundations are missing, people grow up with lacking personality traits, as happened to me.

During adolescence, things did not improve much. I always felt uncomfortable among people, feeling constantly watched or judged. The truly negative turning point occurred in the third year of middle school when, to defend a friend who was being targeted by bullies, I was bullied in turn for an entire year. Something broke inside me. I was no longer the carefree kid I once was, the one who loved adventure and exploring the world to absorb as much as possible from life. On the contrary, I became disillusioned with people, with a melancholic streak quite pronounced in my character. After all, I didn't have much support, and it all boiled down to a few simple words spoken occasionally by some adult. There was never any real attempt at understanding or help, either due to ignorance or the lack of time from those figures who should have understood in time in order to take countermeasures.

Thus, I became a much darker person, increasingly somatizing generalized anxiety in my stomach. Moreover, I carried this sadness with me until high school, albeit in a less marked way.

In my first year of university, however, my social

phobia had intensified to the point that I had to leave my studies and only resumed them later, simply because I couldn't be among people, attend classes, or keep up.

In broad strokes, these were the most significant experiences I had with anxiety, which has always characterized my life, playing an important role in influencing my choices, as well as leading to quite fragile health, the somatization of internal and external problems I faced, along with some traumatic experiences I later encountered.

And perhaps it was precisely these latter

experiences that led me to develop amaxophobia. The first I remember was a near-fatal car accident I had with my family when I was about 15 or 16. My mother swerved with the car, driving us off a slope. We miraculously emerged unscathed: I, my sisters, and she. I never analyzed that event, and over time I believe it etched itself so deeply into my mind that I unconsciously associated the trauma I had experienced with the concept of cars, as if the object itself were a danger.

The event that marked me the most, however, was probably my grandfather's suicide, which occurred when I was 25 years old. From that point on, I began to experience all the symptoms of amaxophobia more intensely. This likely happened because my grandfather shot himself in the car, so again, I associated the car with a traumatic event. For months, I couldn't sleep at night because I was literally in shock.

Even in that case, however, I didn't approach it as a psychological issue in an adequate way; I merely distanced myself from it, trying to create a kind of shield to protect my psyche, dissociating myself from the event.

I never drove; I always delegated to my mother or

others to take me around. I didn't feel capable of taking the car. I was afraid that something bad might happen, especially I couldn't drive with other people in the car. I feared their judgment, being behind the wheel and not being able to drive properly, and then being ridiculed. In short, I felt inadequate.

The more mistakes I made while driving, the more I convinced myself that I shouldn't do it. From there, I began to distance myself from that situation so I wouldn't have to experience it anymore, to avoid those terrible symptoms it caused me. In my mind, I constantly imagined and repeated scenarios that were horrific to me, like parking correctly or letting the car stall on an uphill. I was terrified by these thoughts, but more than anything, I was stopped by the fear of being mocked, reminiscent of the bullying I had endured in middle school. I felt at the mercy of events, just as I had when I was a child. Abandoned, as I had been by my father.

Thus, I had built a comfort zone that I didn't want to detach myself from because it reassured me, even though I often experienced nightmares related to driving.

If it happened that I had to drive for some reason, or even just for a block, I would start to feel physically unwell. The anticipatory anxiety that formed in my mind was so strong that it created very intense physical sensations that were hard to endure: feelings of faintness, shortness of breath, nausea, trembling.

In my case, social phobia, the judgment of others, not feeling capable, and shame were all factors that only fueled my fear. Driving represented personal growth, becoming an adult, taking responsibility, and moving away from family, and I didn't feel ready to face all of this precisely because, in some way, I had already experienced it and had been traumatized.

Over time, it became a fixed thought for me, almost an obsession. On one hand, the desire (in words) to change, and on the other, the lack of courage (in reality) to do so. I felt alone in facing something I saw as huge, an endless mountain to climb. I was David confronting Goliath.

I don't know if there was one main triggering reason or simply the accumulation of all of them, but the fact is that for me, the car represented a kind of metal monster to stay away from.

However, over time, I realized that I could no longer go on like this. This was because I didn't like depending on others; I didn't like being seen as a weak person to be pitied; I no longer liked the sense of inadequacy and shame that resulted in me as a person.

So I decided to try to overcome this fear by gradually confronting it. I first asked my mother to help me with driving, but after a few experiences, I understood that it was better not to rely on her because it was much more damaging than positive, considering that she continued to transmit all her anxieties and fears to me, as she had always done, without understanding how harmful and debilitating they were for me.

I then decided to undertake a psychological path, but that was not much help either because I probably didn't find the right specialist for me to face that specific fear.

I was very ashamed of exposing my problem to friends and relatives, as if it were some kind of physical deformity to be kept well-hidden. So I tried to go it alone and put into practice what I had learned over time, analyzing all the scenarios that occurred and trying to solve them one by one, in small steps. But above all, I realized that to truly resolve the problem, I could not continue to act the same way, as I had always done; on the contrary, I needed a jolt, a breaking point, and from there begin my climb.

HOW TO OVERCOME THE FEAR OF DRIVING: TIPS AND STRATEGIES. WHAT TO DO

Before delving into the core of the book and, more specifically, before outlining the strategies to implement along with useful advice to follow, it would be appropriate to summarize what has been discussed so far in order to gain a clearer overall picture.

As mentioned, fear arises from excessive anxiety and stress that, if not controlled, can turn into panic which, in turn, if chronic, leads to the development of phobia— a type of fear that becomes prolonged and intense, nearly debilitating. It is, therefore, a chained mechanism that starts from an initial cause to reach certain final effects.

The underlying anxiety can be of two types:

normal, thus having a positive value when it serves to avoid real danger, or pathological when it creates perpetual states of alarm that are essentially unnecessary, based on personal ideas that are not closely related to the reality of facts.

The anxiety underlying phobia is, in fact, anticipatory, generated by mental projections and fantasies that arise and develop as symptoms of other discomforts.

The mechanism that every human mind employs to counteract the previous points and protect its well-being is based on the fight or flight reaction.

This behavior is entirely normal when it occurs under specific circumstances and returns to control after the threat has subsided, while it becomes a dysfunctional attitude when it is managed by fear itself and not by the individual.

Thus, the phobic individual tries to create a safe zone, the so-called comfort zone, in which they can better manage anxiety and distance themselves from thoughts that cause the typical symptoms of phobias when a person feels threatened in their safety, both physically since such symptoms are just the extremization of anxiety signals, and psychologically when they evoke feelings such as discomfort, nervousness, frustration, behavioral issues, and other unpleasant reactions stemming from the psychic sphere.

These thoughts are atavistic, derived from developmental processes our species has implemented to safeguard itself over millennia and have remained rooted in us, even though the human and social contexts we live in have changed, along with the related dangers we face today, leading individuals to confront new stress stimuli which they often struggle to manage properly.

This has resulted in the development of numerous phobias, including amaxophobia (the fear of driving). The latter can stem from trauma, low self-esteem, insecurity, lack of confidence in one's abilities, personalities that seek to control external events because they are terrified of the consequences, the judgment of others, the resulting sense of shame, the inability to confront it properly, and even cultural prejudices such as the belief that women have more problems driving compared to men or, conversely, that men must always be strong and virile and not experience such discomfort, thus creating a stigma for those who face this issue, diminishing them as a woman or a man.

There is, thus, a tendency to postpone the solution to the problem, to delegate to others, seeking someone to save us from ourselves, becoming totally dependent because avoidance leads to not facing the situation, which consequently limits one's life and results in regression as an individual, for on one hand, one does not grow or develop their adult personality, while on the other, the comfort zone (a barrier separating the individual from the world, from the community) that is created becomes a sort of bubble, a shell that prevents anything from penetrating from the outside, causing the personal sphere to remain uncontaminated by the social sphere and vice versa, remaining trapped in the usual mechanisms because it cannot develop and consider an alternative to the habitual personal behavior it is accustomed to, which is the only way it knows.

The situations that cause the most discomfort, as noted, include: driving alone, driving in traffic, driving on unfamiliar roads, etc. Therefore, a whole series of scenarios are created that feed and justify one's fears.

Having clearly understood what lies at the root of fear and why our body implements specific defense strategies, we can now move on to understanding how to address the problem as a whole, outlining what must be done and what should instead be limited as it generates anxiety.

If we continue to repeat the same actions or reactions, we will inevitably end up achieving the same results. This is almost a mathematical concept. It may change slightly, but fundamentally, one will remain in the same situation.

Thus, this chain must be broken so as not to

perpetuate the vicious cycle at its foundation.

The very first thing you need to do is enter a mental state of real correction because the will to succeed is the essential component to embark on any healing journey, as is the positive thinking that underlies every change, when you believe in what you are doing and are convinced it will yield results. After all, trying may result in failure, while not trying means that you have already failed in some way. Even not deciding is a decision, and often it is the worst one you can make, because it does not allow you to address any issue, while at the same time time has passed, that very time you could have used to heal, and above all because no situation resolves itself by leaving it pending. However, the idea that should be at the foundation is not so much about the time that has passed without taking action, as that is an aspect that cannot be changed anymore, and because it was likely the time you needed to stand still and figure out what you actually want to do or be in life. What really matters is day zero, meaning the day you decide to concretely change, which serves as an actual starting point to solve this problem. You must think that in everything, there is a probability of success, especially when you have set a goal to achieve, and you must pursue that path despite the difficulties that you will encounter along the way.

Do not delegate the solution of the problem to others and do not rely too much on hoping that someone from above will save you because the only person who can do that is you. It is fine to ask someone for help if a problem seems too big to confront, but the mistake that often arises is expecting that person to do the work for you. It will never happen because if it is your problem, only you can solve it for yourself.

Do not let it become an obsession, and at the

same time, do not force yourself not to think about it too much, because the more you try not to think about a certain thing, the more you will end up falling into that very thought. It is the concept well expressed by George Lakoff with the phrase "Don't think about the elephant." As soon as you finish reading, I am sure that you started to think of just an elephant. If you impose yourself not to think about it anymore, you will inevitably continue to do so. Just as you try not to think about amaxophobia, it will cyclically and constantly reappear in your mind.

Do not see it as something unsolvable, but rather

adopt the perspective that it is a temporary situation, just like the anxiety you are experiencing, and that if you decide to solve it, then you will truly solve it. It all depends on you.

Do not postpone until tomorrow what you can face today. Even a simple gesture indicates a concrete effort to change. Procrastination only feeds the idea that you will not make it. Show yourself and the problem that you are ready to succeed.

Start not to feel judged if you are not good at something. Shake off the mental projections, both your own and those from others, or those you perceive as such (after all, the world does not think about you, and just as people judge you, you can also do the same with them if such a situation arises, especially since human beings thrive on this). Begin to understand that not being able to do something well does not qualify you as a person or as a failure. Focus on what you do well to gain more self-confidence and relate it to amaxophobia, thinking that one day you will be able to drive well just as you are able to do something else well now.

Do not label yourself to gain sympathy and be

seen as a victim. Do not complain about the problem or about being misunderstood. It is humanly understandable that a person who has not experienced your same discomfort may find it difficult to realize. Therefore, try to understand their incomprehension towards you and do not expect the opposite to happen.

Try not to be too much of a perfectionist and start to understand that things cannot be controlled. Let yourself be carried away by events and face them when they present themselves to you. Self-esteem is fundamental.

Do not hide the problem because in doing so, over time, it will only wear you out inside, especially if you are ashamed of it because you will give it more weight than it actually has and consequently more power to harm you. On the contrary, expose it, metabolize it, and live it. Try to exorcise it and define it for what it actually is.

Do not allow this fear to become a monster that you cannot face. Do not view it as an elephant that can crush you at any moment, but try to shrink it until it becomes a mouse that you can chase away whenever you want. Face the fear.

Fear is not rational; it is an alarm bell. Try to understand that this sense of alertness is something positive and not something to fight against. Expand your comfort zone to include the car. Our mind tends to see things in the short and medium term, so it does not want to confront the peak of anxiety that lies ahead, which is why it tends to block you from the start. Therefore, you must go beyond this projection because, as I explained earlier, sooner or later it will pass; it is physiological. So try to live those sensations, as hard and unpleasant as they may be, without holding onto them, but rather letting yourself go because, on one hand, sooner or later you will get used to it, and on the other hand, by doing this, you will manage to overcome them more easily because you will no longer create a counter-force opposing a force that fuels physical and mental tension, making them more enduring. In other words, experience a brief period of intense anxiety rather than a prolonged, but less intense one to avoid it becoming chronic.

Imagine yourself happy at the wheel, substituting negative and disturbing thoughts with calming thoughts. Positive thoughts, in fact, combat irrational ones. You are the one driving the car, not the other way around; you have full control over your actions, and by being attentive to others, you also limit their actions because they cannot harm you in any way. You reduce the probability of this happening, especially because you are not at the mercy of events but know how to handle any situation that arises.

Avoid avoidance, and instead, seek exposure to the problem by tackling it in small steps as often as possible. You don't have to burden yourself with difficult and unattainable goals but instead aim for many small milestones that you can easily pursue and achieve. This concept is fundamental because it starts from breaking down a large problem (or one seen as such) to create many small segments of the problem that can actually be solved. In the end, you will end up solving the entirety.

Finally, the practical solution to amaxophobia is based on a method. In fact, you need to adopt a precise protocol during which you will note the progress made and the fears encountered, along with their intensity, and particularly, you need to follow seven steps.

These last steps have a subjective duration, and you should only move on to the next step when you feel ready to do so. So give yourself all the time you need to start controlling your anxiety in this situation;

first step: simply sit in the car, on the driver's side, and begin to familiarize yourself with the vehicle. Start by not seeing it as the metal monster it seems to be, but rather as the object, the means of transportation that it actually is, which you need to move around and be free. Touch the steering wheel, the gearbox, press the clutch, brake, and accelerator pedals. Do things that do not cause you anxiety, such as, for example, reading a book or listening to music, but do it in the car so that you associate normal behaviors with driving;

second step: start the car and shift gears until the anxiety from this action decreases. Put it in first, second, third, fourth, and fifth gear. Then do the same thing in reverse, meaning from fifth gear back to first, downshifting through all the gears. Then put it in reverse;

third step: drive a short stretch of road, perhaps with someone beside you if it helps reduce your stress. A controlled initial drive, in other words, that can help you unblock yourself while becoming more familiar with the vehicle and your feelings. This can be done on a secluded road or in a parking lot;

fourth step: park. Start with simpler maneuvers, and get into the mindset of taking the proper measurements of your car and those around you, as well as any obstacles you might encounter along the way;

fifth step: start driving on the road for longer distances. Until you face a bypass road and eventually also a highway;

sixth step: tackle unfamiliar routes, especially busy roads. Start driving alone and do it frequently;

seventh step: face the final test, which is starting on an incline with a line of vehicles behind you. I believe this is one of the most anxiety-inducing situations while driving, and for this reason, it would be an excellent test to assess your level of anxiety and how you manage it. It is simply a symbolic test: if this is not what causes you the most anxiety, try to confront what you believe does and carefully evaluate how you feel doing it."

To avoid regressing, you need to implement these exercises daily. Driving daily (at a pace you're comfortable with) is helpful because it's a form of training. Just like a runner trains for a marathon by monitoring the signals from their body and their mental preparation, you must do the same for driving. It's exactly the same thing.

Another piece of advice I can offer is to start a psychotherapy journey, particularly cognitive-behavioral therapy, which can provide you with all the necessary tools to better confront your phobia. This involves understanding the underlying cause of your discomfort, allowing you to follow general guidelines and apply them to your specific situation.

An important practice to implement is breathing techniques, as they directly stimulate the vagus nerve. Diaphragmatic breathing, in particular, has proven useful in activating this nerve. In a perpetual state of alertness, this nerve becomes overstimulated and overloaded, sending excessive signals to the body. The function of this nerve is fundamental in many disorders, some of which may seem unrelated, ranging from tachycardia to gastrointestinal issues, as well as stress and respiratory problems.

Essentially, the pneumogastric nerve, or as it's commonly known, the vagus nerve (its name is no accident, as it travels a long path in the body innervating various organs—hence it "wanders" throughout the body)—has numerous branches (smaller nerves) that reach the heart, lungs, stomach, ears, and other organs such as the liver, spleen, kidneys, and pancreas. It is the main representative of the nerve fibers comprising the parasympathetic nervous system. The vagus nerve serves various functions: it stimulates calmness, relaxation, rest, and digestion.

This illustrates why it is so important and how it can influence our health, as it is literally the regulator of stress, which in turn is the foundation of phobias.

In conclusion, carefully analyze the repercussions and discomfort this disorder causes in your life, giving it a degree of intensity. It is crucial to be motivated and convinced of the necessity to overcome it, since in most cases it limits personal autonomy, lifestyle, and the psychosocial well-being of the individual experiencing it. One shouldn't focus on how to control the car, but rather on how to put a brake on anxious thoughts. This is the crux of the problem.

It is also important to learn how to counter and

rationalize the dysfunctional thoughts associated with the feared situation. You should begin to work towards normalized driving, viewing it as a possible goal to achieve rather than something unattainable. For this reason, it is essential to confront the fear, not only by changing the underlying thoughts that fuel it but also by gradually exposing oneself to feared situations (starting with those that generate less anxiety) and then increasing exposure and difficulty, facing the more traumatic ones. Every small step will be a small success, boosting confidence and security to face the next step more consciously.

As is the case with most anxiety disorders, practical advice, if implemented, provides valuable support in overcoming fear. However, depending on the characteristics and severity of the disorder, as previously mentioned, the assistance of a professional specialized in phobias can be very helpful. Among the types of therapy that can be practiced are:

Cognitive-behavioral therapy. This psychological approach aims to change those negative and limiting thoughts associated with driving.

Hypnosis. This practice can lead to a state of

relaxation that helps the individual recognize the causes of their fears and therefore overcome them more easily.

Systematic desensitization. This method aims to address each belief related to driving one at a time, gradually dismantling each until achieving total desensitization.

CONCLUSIONS

We have finally reached the conclusion of this

discussion. Writing this book was almost a necessity, both to put in writing everything I have experienced, particularly my thoughts, fears, and anxieties, so as to exorcise and confront them better (considering that the mind tends to record everything that happens to it, archiving information like in a database), and to try to help those who are experiencing the same issues that I have faced.

I have not completely overcome the problem, but I am nevertheless satisfied with the milestone I have reached, namely, autonomy in driving and managing anxiety. With commitment and willpower, I will succeed in completely exorcising the discomfort, making it normal, and no longer allowing it to influence me. I am 80% along the path and 20% from the solution.

There are indeed many of us in this situation, and it is very disheartening to think that often there is a lack of a proper method to address it, as we are essentially left to fend for ourselves. It's demoralizing but also a starting point for reacting, almost like a spring that snaps inside you, prompting you to resist what doesn't work and what you dislike. For every action, there is an equal or opposite reaction. In this case, it must be equal in strength and opposite to counter it.

In hindsight, I realize I could have written a technical, very verbose book so that I could say I had written a "scientific" manual, but what good would that have done? If not to satisfy my ego, it would have provided little to no benefit to those preparing to read it, offering difficult concepts that are ultimately forgettable. Big words and useless convolutions, which hardly imprint themselves on the reader's memory.

On the contrary, I chose to use colloquial language that is easy to understand, allowing for a wider and smoother assimilation of the key concepts that have been carefully highlighted and, at times, even repeated for better imprinting.

I have revisited the various emotional states that have characterized these years of my life, seeking to analyze the various potential causes underlying them, allowing for a 360-degree comparison, as well as complete intellectual honesty, without hiding in any situation or pretending to be someone I am not. From these reflections stems a certain regret for having inevitably lost part of my life because it was limited by driving anxiety, with the awareness that the years spent procrastinating will never come back.

This is a state of mind common to anyone who feels deprived, due to their own negligence or circumstances beyond their control, of precious and vital time. At the same time, however, it must represent a starting point for change. Indeed, while this bitter realization is true, on the other hand, I can only be grateful to confront it because what doesn't kill you makes you stronger, and because human existence is made up of experiences, not always positive.

After all, mental strength is everything when it

comes to effectively confronting unpleasant situations that life throws at us, and in doing so, it ends up enhancing a person's adaptive value. And this means growing up and maturing.

In this case, I address you, dear reader, do not allow this fear to destroy you; do not let it harm you any longer.

A heartfelt thank you for purchasing and reading this book. I genuinely hope that you can find relief and resolve this issue as soon as possible. In this regard, I wish you all the best.

A big hug.

O.I.P.L.

CONTACTS

parlaconoltre@gmail.com

YouTube: Oltre i propri limiti

Telegram: Oltre1991